The Story of Pegasus

Retold by
Susanna Davidson

Illustrated by Simona Bursi

Reading consultant: Alison Kelly
Roehampton University

D1514879

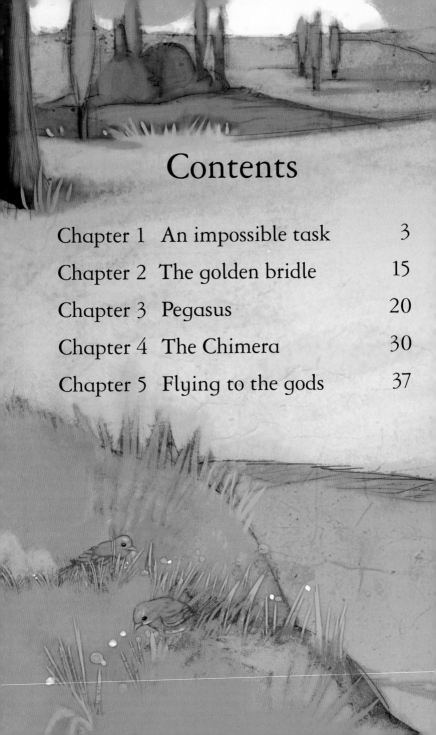

Contents

Chapter 1   An impossible task   3

Chapter 2   The golden bridle   15

Chapter 3   Pegasus   20

Chapter 4   The Chimera   30

Chapter 5   Flying to the gods   37

Chapter 1

An impossible task

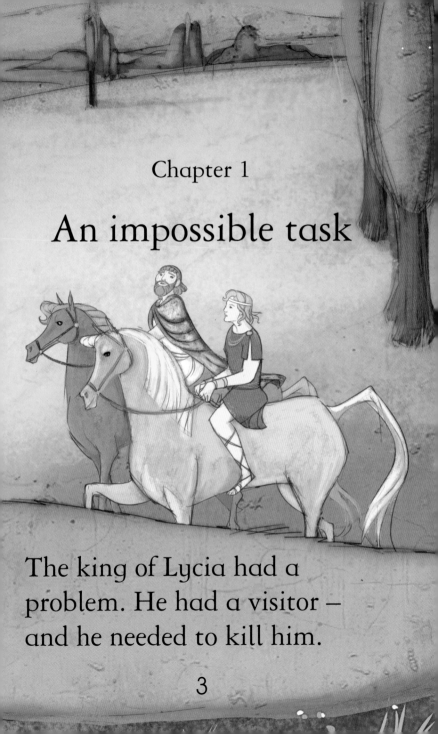

The king of Lycia had a
problem. He had a visitor –
and he needed to kill him.

The visitor was a young man named Bellerophon. He had arrived with a letter from the king's son-in-law. The letter said...

When he stayed with us, Bellerophon was very rude to my wife – your daughter. I want you to kill him.

King Proteus

The king worried for days.
"I can't do it," he thought. "I
can't kill a guest."

Instead, he decided to set
Bellerophon an impossible task.

"There's a terrible creature in my kingdom," said the king one night. "It's called the Chimera. I want you to kill it."

Bellerophon gulped. He couldn't say no to the king. But the Chimera breathed fire and had the head of a lion...

the body
of a goat...

...and a snake
for a tail.

It was deadly. Lots of men
had tried to kill it before.

All of them had failed.

Bellerophon set out the next day, scared it would be his last.

"How will I ever kill the Chimera?" he wondered aloud.

"You can't do it alone," declared a voice.

Bellerophon jumped. A wizened old man had suddenly appeared.

"He's a flying horse with feathery white wings, who swoops through the air like a bird."

"But no one has ever ridden him before."

"How do I catch him?" asked Bellerophon, his eyes shining.

"You'll need the help of the gods," the old man replied.

"See the temple on the hill? Sleep there tonight and help will come to you."

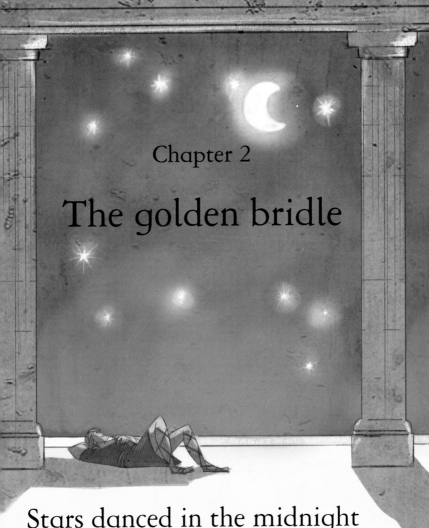

Chapter 2

The golden bridle

Stars danced in the midnight sky. The moon shone brightly. Bellerophon closed his eyes and dreamed...

A goddess stood before him.
"I am Athena," she said, in a
low, musical voice.

"Take this golden bridle. Go
to Mount Helicon and wait for
the winged horse."

"Place this bridle over his head, and you will be able to ride him."

"Now, sleep until morning comes," she added, gently brushing his eyelids.

17

The goddess had gone when Bellerophon awoke. But the golden bridle was still there, glittering in his hands.

"Pegasus could be mine!" gasped Bellerophon. And he set out for Mount Helicon.

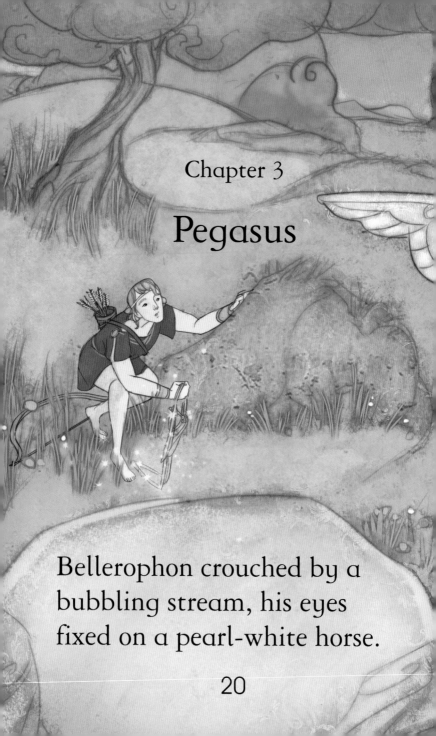

Chapter 3

Pegasus

Bellerophon crouched by a bubbling stream, his eyes fixed on a pearl-white horse.

The horse bent his head
to drink. His golden hooves
sparkled in the morning sun.

Bellerophon crept forward.
His bare feet padded silently
across the soft grass.

Quick as a flash, Bellerophon
slipped the bridle over the
horse's head.

Pegasus reared up, beating
the air with his powerful wings.

Bellerophon clung tight to the reins. He whispered words of calm to Pegasus.

The horse gave a whinny and dropped to the ground.

"You're mine now," said Bellerophon. "Let's ride together."

He swung himself onto Pegasus' back. The horse grew calmer still.

"It must be a magic bridle," realized Bellerophon. Proudly, he stroked Pegasus' silky neck. "Take to the skies!" he commanded.

Pegasus leaped into the air
and they soared higher and
higher, over treetops and hills...

...over mountains,
through clouds and
up into the airy blue.

Bellerophon guided Pegasus
to the rocky land where the
monstrous Chimera lived.

Even from the
sky, he could see it
clearly, belching
smoke and fire.

Pegasus hovered above the Chimera on beating wings. It was time to attack.

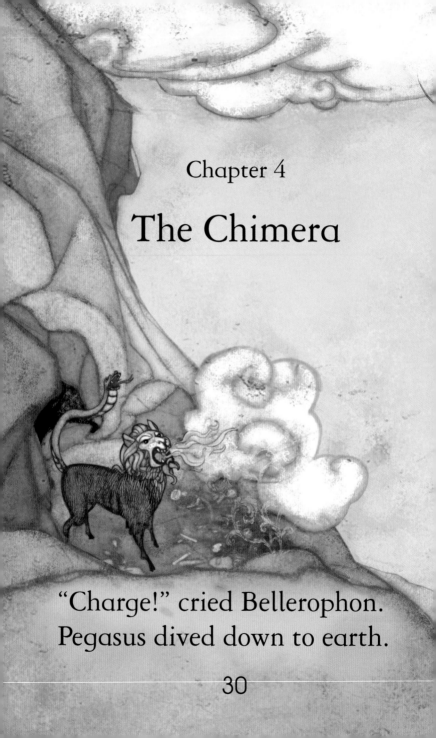

Chapter 4

The Chimera

"Charge!" cried Bellerophon.
Pegasus dived down to earth.

The wind whipped through
Bellerophon's hair as he raised
his bow and arrow. He aimed
at the lion's head... and fired.

The Chimera roared in anger.
It leaped out of the way and
shot out a blast
of flames.

Bellerophon pulled Pegasus back to the safety of the skies and aimed his arrow again. This time it hit home, piercing the Chimera's side.

Now the creature was angrier than ever. Its snake's head spat venom at Bellerophon.

He twisted away, just in time. Then he urged Pegasus to spin around, swooping down at the Chimera with his spear at the ready.

As the Chimera opened its mouth to breath fire, Bellerophon plunged his spear deep into the monster's throat.

The spear melted in the fiery heat. The Chimera struggled, choked and gasped...

It rose up in one last effort, then slumped to the ground, dead at last.

Chapter 5

Flying to the gods

"I have done the impossible,"
Bellerophon told the king.

"I have tamed Pegasus, and together we killed the Chimera, just as you asked."

The king was amazed. "People everywhere will thank you," he said.

And they did. Bellerophon became famous across the land. "You're a hero," they shouted from the streets. "You killed the Chimera. You're like a god!"

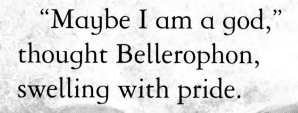

"Maybe I am a god,"
thought Bellerophon,
swelling with pride.

"After all, I have a horse that
can fly... I can kill monsters
where other men fail..."

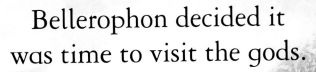

Bellerophon decided it was time to visit the gods.

He swung himself onto Pegasus and they flew to the highest mountain of all.

Zeus, king of the gods, saw Bellerophon coming. "How dare he?" he thundered.

"No human should ever come to the land of the gods."

He sent down an insect to sting Pegasus, who bucked and reared. Bellerophon tumbled through the sky.

Zeus watched him fall. Then he caught Pegasus and rode him home to Mount Olympus.

From that day, Pegasus
lived with the gods, carrying
thunderbolts for Zeus.

Bellerophon crashed back to earth. He landed in a dazed, miserable heap.

No one would go near him, now his pride had angered the gods. He was left to wander alone, for the rest of his days.

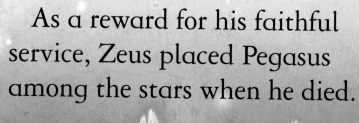

As a reward for his faithful service, Zeus placed Pegasus among the stars when he died.

You can still see him
there today.

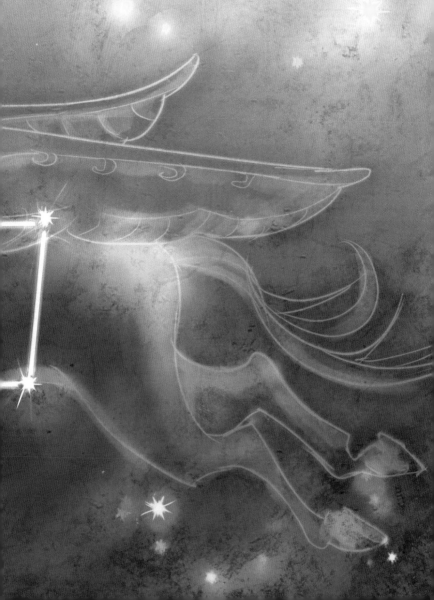

Pegasus, the Flying Horse

The story of Pegasus is a myth from Ancient Greece. Legend says that he sprang from the neck of a monster named Medusa, after another hero, Perseus, cut off her head. Pegasus lived wild in a forest until he was captured by Bellerophon.

Usborne Quicklinks

For links to websites where you can find out more about Greek myths and hear how Ancient Greek names are pronounced, go to the Usborne Quicklinks Website at **www.usborne-quicklinks.com** and enter the keyword 'Pegasus'.

Please follow the internet safety guidelines on the Usborne Quicklinks Website. Usborne Publishing cannot be responsible for the content of any website other than its own.

History consultant: Dr. Anne Millard
Designed by Michelle Lawrence
Digital design: Nick Wakeford
Series editor: Lesley Sims
Series designer: Russell Punter

First published in 2011 by Usborne Publishing Ltd., Usborne House, 83-85 Saffron Hill, London EC1N 8RT, England. www.usborne.com
Copyright © 2011 Usborne Publishing Ltd.

All rights reserved. No part of this publication may be reproduced, stored in a retrieval system or transmitted in any form or by any means, electronic, mechanical, photocopying, recording or otherwise, without the prior permission of the publisher. The name Usborne and the devices ♀⊕ are Trade Marks of Usborne Publishing Ltd. UE First published in America in 2011.